INTRODUCTION

WHAT IS A SUPER HERO?

You might think of super heroes as daring guys with flowing capes who are able to do super human feats like fly over buildings, bend metal with their bare hands and see through closed doors.

You probably love to dress up and pretend to be a super hero, but at the same time you think, "I can never be a *real* super hero". Well, this book is here to tell you that you can be a super hero and that the kind of super hero you can be is more awesome than the one with the flowing cape, bulging muscles and eye mask.

You can be a super hero for Jesus! Through the stories in the **Super Heroes Storybook** you will learn the kind of traits that real super heroes have – super heroes for Jesus. Moses was a brave and obedient leader who led the people through the Red Sea on dry ground. David was a young boy who stood up to and defeated a giant. Noah built a boat and made it through the flood and into a new world. Each of these men obeyed God, each was brave and each was a super hero for Jesus.

A true super hero doesn't have bulging muscles and supernatural powers, a true super hero has faith in Jesus and the courage to obey Him and do His will.

Through the pages of this book you will learn that you too can be a super hero for Jesus. **ARE YOU READY FOR AN ADVENTURE?**

SUPER HERO ADAM

THE VERY FIRST MAN

Based on Genesis 2

In the beginning, there was nothing to hear and nothing to see. There was no world. No sun or moon or stars. No people. No plants. No animals. Then God started making things. He made the earth. He made the land and the oceans. God made the sun, the moon and thousands of stars. God made all kinds of animals to live on the land and in the waters. He made great big elephants and tiny little monkeys. He made whales and seahorses to swim in the oceans. He also made birds to fly in the sky.

God made lots of things, but He wasn't finished. God saved His best creation for last. That was the very first man! God made Adam out of plain old dust from the ground. God made Adam in His own image. That means Adam could think and make decisions – just as God does. He could do work and he could take care of the animals. God made a beautiful place for Adam to live. **THEN HE GAVE ADAM A SPECIAL JOB TO DO.** He asked Adam to give names to all the animals. So Adam decided to call a giraffe a giraffe. He named tigers, eagles and all the other things God had made. Adam was busy, but he was also lonely. He needed another person to talk with and help him with the work. So God made Adam fall asleep. Then He took a rib from Adam's side and made the very first woman. Her name was Eve. They were the beginning of all people!

SUPER HERO CHARACTERISTIC

Adam was the very first person God created and He was created amazingly in God's image. He was the first super hero to care for animals and nature.

SUPER HERO TIP

Adam was special because he was the first man God made and he was made in God's image. YOU are special too, because you are also made in God's image! You can think. You can make choices. You can be kind and loving. You can do any job God gives you to do!

The LORD God formed the man from the dust of the ground. He breathed the breath of life into the man's nostrils, and the man became a living person.

Genesis 2:7

2 SUPER HERO NOAH

A BRAVE STORMY SEA ADVENTURER

Based on Genesis 6-9

Many years after God made Adam and Eve people stopped caring about God. They didn't obey Him. They just did whatever they wanted. That made God sad. He tried to make them understand that they would be happier if they obeyed Him and got along with each other. But the people wouldn't listen. So God decided to start over with creation. He sent a big flood that destroyed everything He had made – all the plants and animals and even all the people on earth, except Noah. God saved Noah and his family, because **NOAH WAS THE ONLY ONE WHO STILL OBEYED GOD**.

"A big flood is coming. I want you to build a boat," God told Noah. "Your family will be safe from the flood when you go inside the boat. I will send animals to go in the boat too." Noah's neighbors made fun of him for building the boat. But Noah obeyed God. He kept working on the boat. When it was finished God sent two of every kind of animal to go inside it. Noah and his family went in the boat too. Sure enough the big flood came. It wiped out everything. But Noah's family and the animals were saved from the flood, because Noah obeyed God.

When the flood was over, God put a rainbow in the sky as a sign of His promise to never send a flood that would destroy everything again. Noah and his family started new lives in the new world. Soon there were more people and more animals – all because Noah obeyed God!

13

SUPER HERO CHARACTERISTIC

Noah showed courage when he obeyed God despite being mocked and laughed at. He had the courage to do what no man had done before, to venture out in a boat with a lot of noisy and excited animals! He trusted God to take care of him.

SUPER HERO TIP

It isn't always easy to obey God.
Your friends may tease you or make fun of you.
But obeying God is the only way to please Him.
It is most important.

Those who obey
God's word truly
show how completely
they love Him.

1 John 2:5

FROM PRISON TO PHARAOH'S PALACE

Based on Genesis 37, 39-46

Joseph had eleven brothers. That could have been fun, except they didn't like Joseph at all. They were jealous of him because their dad liked him better than all of them. Joseph's dad even gave him a fancy, colorful coat! It was nicer than any of their clothes. That made Joseph feel pretty important. Joseph had some dreams that he was going to be more important than any of his brothers someday too. His brothers didn't like that either. They decided to get rid of Joseph. When some slave traders came near where they were working, they sold Joseph to them. They lied to their dad and said that a wild animal had killed him. Joseph was taken to Egypt where he became a slave. He was working for his owner when he was thrown in prison for something he didn't do!

BUT GOD WAS WATCHING OUT FOR JOSEPH. He helped Joseph help the king of Egypt. The king took Joseph out of prison and made him a ruler in Egypt. God told Joseph that a drought was coming and there would be no food. So Joseph came up with a plan to save food for Egypt.

People from other countries came to buy food from him. They would starve if Joseph didn't sell them food. One day Joseph's brothers came. They didn't recognize him, but he knew who they were. Joseph remembered all the mean things they had done to him. He remembered that they sold him to the slave traders. Joseph could have put them in jail. He could have killed them. He didn't though. Joseph forgave his brothers for all they had done to him. He had them stay in Egypt and he took care of all of them.

SUPER HERO CHARACTERISTIC

Joseph forgave others, even when it was really difficult. He knew that God had a plan through all that happened to him.

SUPER HERO TIP

Joseph's story is a good lesson: Forgiving others instead of trying to get even with them is the super hero way that pleases God. Always try to forgive your friends when they are mean to you. Don't try to take revenge.

"Even if that person wrongs you seven times a day and each time turns again and asks forgiveness, you must forgive."

Luke 17:4

SUPER HERO MOSES

4

A STRONG LEADER

Based on Exodus 3-14

Many years later the Israelites became slaves in Egypt. It wasn't fun. The Egyptians were mean. The Israelites begged God to rescue them and He answered their prayers. He sent Moses.

"Lead My people out of Egypt, Moses. I don't want them to be slaves anymore," God said. Moses was nervous. He wasn't sure he could do it. But God promised to help him.

God sent ten terrible plagues on the Egyptians. After each one, Moses went to the Pharaoh of Egypt and said, "God says to let His people go!" Nine times Pharaoh said, "No." Finally, after the tenth plague, Pharoah let the Israelites leave and Moses led the people out of Egypt. One night they set up camp on the shore of the Red Sea. But then they saw Pharaoh's army coming after them. He had changed his mind! He wanted his slaves back in Egypt!

There was no way to escape. The Red Sea was behind them and the Egyptian army was in front of them. "Why did you lead us out of Egypt? Now Pharaoh will make us work harder than ever!" the people complained to Moses.

BUT MOSES WASN'T SCARED. "DON'T BE AFRAID. WATCH WHAT GOD DOES," HE SAID. He held his shepherd's staff over the water of the Red Sea. God sent a strong wind blowing across the water. Pretty soon the water blew into two big walls with dry ground between them. God held the water back while every single Israelite crossed through the sea safely. The Egyptians tried to follow, but God let the waters crash down on them. The Israelite people were safe!

SUPER HERO CHARACTERISTIC

Moses was a strong and fearless leader. He led the Israelites out of Egypt. Even when he wasn't sure what to do he trusted God to help him.

SUPER HERO TIP

God asked Moses to lead the people.
He gave him the courage and power to do the job.
When God gives you a job to do, He will give
you the power to do it!

Those who trust in the LORD
will find new strength. They will
soar high on wings like eagles.
They will run and not grow weary.
They will walk and not faint.

Isaiah 40:31

5

SUPER HERO MOSES

GOD'S MIGHTY MESSENGER

Based on Exodus 20:1-17

It had been two months since Moses led the Israelites out of Egypt. Moses was leading the people to the land God promised to give them as their new home. Sometimes the people got tired on the long trip and complained to Moses. They also complained when they ran out of food and when they couldn't find water. Each time they complained, Moses asked God for help and God always helped them. He even did miracles to keep them safe. But the next time they were scared the people quickly forgot how God was watching out for them.

One time the people were camped near a big mountain called Mount Sinai. **GOD CALLED MOSES TO COME UP THE MOUNTAIN AND MEET WITH HIM.** He had to come by himself so Moses told the people to wait for him. God had special rules that He wanted the people to know, but He wouldn't speak to all the people. He told the rules to Moses and Moses took them to the people. These rules are called the Ten Commandments. God wrote the rules on pieces of stone and Moses took them to the people. If the people would pay attention to these rules it would help them get along with each other and obey God.

THE TEN COMMANDMENTS:

1. Worship only God.
2. Do not worship idols.
3. Be careful how you use God's name.
4. Keep God's day holy.
5. Respect your father and mother.
6. Do not murder.
7. Keep your marriage pure.
8. Do not steal.
9. Do not lie about anyone.
10. Do not want what other people have.

25

SUPER HERO CHARACTERISTIC

Moses was a mighty messenger for God. He told the Israelites what God wanted them to do. Moses received the Ten Commandments and we still live by them today.

SUPER HERO TIP

God gives His messages to people in different ways. He speaks through His Word and sometimes God delivers His messages through people. Pay attention to the messages God gives you. He might have a message for you to share with others!

"If you love Me, obey My commandments."
John 14:15

6

SUPER HEROES CALEB AND JOSHUA

TWO MEN WITH A ROCK-SOLID FAITH IN GOD

Based on Numbers 13-14

Moses led the Israelites out of Egypt. He led them out of slavery. God had promised them freedom and a land they could call their own. They walked for a long time and finally, they reached the land of Canaan. This was the land God promised to give them way back when they left Egypt. Yes, God had PROMISED to give them this land to be their homeland. But, there were people already living there so the Israelites would have to fight them – and win – to be able take over the land.

Moses sent twelve spies into Canaan to see what the land was like. When they returned ten of the spies said, "Yes, the land is beautiful. It grows wonderful plants. We would never be hungry there. But the people who live there are giants. We could never defeat them! We should just forget about this land. We could never win."

THE TWO OTHER SPIES, CALEB AND JOSHUA, TRUSTED GOD. They said, "Look, God promised us this land. It is already ours! He will help us win, even against giants! Let's get going!" The people listened to what the ten scared spies had to say. They also listened to what Caleb and Joshua said. But the people didn't trust God enough to believe He would help them win. They didn't even believe He would do another miracle to help them. So the people decided to believe the ten doubters instead of Caleb and Joshua. They decided they couldn't try to take the land of Canaan. God punished the people because they didn't trust Him. Their punishment was that they had to wander around in the wilderness for forty years instead of going into their new homeland!

SUPER HERO CHARACTERISTIC

Caleb and Joshua believed God would do what He promised. They had a strong and firm faith in God. They believed in a great and mighty God who could do the impossible.

SUPER HERO TIP

When God says He is going to do something –
believe Him – even if it seems impossible!
He always keeps His word.

*God is faithful to
do what He says.*
1 Corinthians 1:9

SUPER HERO JOSHUA

A MIGHTY AND FEARLESS WARRIOR

Based on Joshua 6

The Israelites were camped outside the city of Jericho. It was the biggest city in the land of Canaan – the land that God promised to give them to be their new home. Jericho was protected by big, thick walls that completely surrounded the city. The gates of the wall were locked up tight. No one could go in or out. How would Joshua's army get inside?

Never fear. God had a plan. After all, He had promised the land to them. **"JOSHUA, I WILL HELP YOU CAPTURE THE CITY OF JERICHO," GOD SAID. "DO EXACTLY WHAT I TELL YOU TO DO."**

God told Joshua to do this: "March your army all around the city of Jericho once a day for six days. The priests should go first. They should carry their horns, but they can't blow them. All of your soldiers must be completely silent while they march. On the seventh day march them around the city seven times. On the seventh time have the soldiers give a great shout while the priests blow their trumpets. When they do the big walls around the city will just fall down."

Joshua did exactly what God said. While the army marched in silence around the city, the people of Jericho made fun of them and laughed at them. But, on the seventh time around when the soldiers shouted, the walls around Jericho crashed to the ground! Joshua's army rushed into Jericho and captured the whole city!

SUPER HERO CHARACTERISTIC

Joshua was very good at listening and doing. Joshua followed God's instructions exactly. He led the people to the city and commanded them to do just what God instructed him to do.

SUPER HERO TIP

When God gives you instructions (and the Bible is full of instructions) it is very important to follow those instructions exactly. Don't try to add your own instructions to what God says. Obey Him and see what wonderful things He does for you!

Teach me to do Your will, for You are my God.

Psalm 143:10

SUPER HERO SAMSON

THE STRONG MAN

Based on Judges 13-16

When Samson was born his parents dedicated him to God's service. **SAMSON GREW UP TO BE THE STRONGEST MAN IN THE WORLD.** God helped him do amazing miracles showing His strength.

The Philistines were God's enemies. They wanted to capture Samson. So they made a deal with Samson's girlfriend, Delilah. "Find out what makes Samson so strong. Help us capture him and we will give you a reward." Delilah begged Samson to tell her where his strength came from. "If I were tied up with seven brand-new bowstrings, I would not be able to escape," Samson said. So Delilah tied Samson up and called the Philistines, but Samson broke the bowstrings and escaped.

"Come on, tell me where your strength comes from," Delilah begged. Samson told her that if he were tied up with new ropes he would not be able to escape. Of course, Delilah tied him up and called for the Philistines. Samson snapped the ropes like they were strings and escaped. "You're making fun of me!" Delilah complained. But Samson lied to her again. Finally Delilah said, "If you really love me you will tell me the truth." That got to Samson so he told the truth – if his hair were cut his strength would be gone. As soon as he fell asleep, Delilah called the Philistines and they cut Samson's hair and captured him.

Samson felt terrible. "I'm sorry I disobeyed. Give me strength to defeat Your enemies once more – even if I die with them," he prayed. God gave Samson strength to push apart the big pillars holding up the building where the Philistines were. It fell down, killing all the Philistines inside. Samson died that day, but he defeated God's enemies!

SUPER HERO CHARACTERISTIC

Samson was super strong. He used his mighty strength to defeat the Israelites' enemy, the Philistines.

SUPER HERO TIP

Obeying God means He is on your side and that means you will have super hero strength from Him too! With God on your side you can beat any problem.

God is our refuge and strength, always ready to help in times of trouble.

Psalm 46:1

SUPERSONIC HEARING

Based on 1 Samuel 3

Samuel was just a young boy when he went to live in the temple so that Eli, the priest, could teach him how to serve God. One night Samuel was in bed when he heard someone call his name, "Samuel!" He jumped out of bed and ran to see what Eli wanted. But Eli was asleep. It wasn't Eli who had called. So Samuel went back to bed. He was nearly asleep when he heard his name called again. "Samuel! Samuel!" Right away the young boy jumped out of bed and ran to Eli again. He asked what he could do for the old priest.

But once again Eli said, "Go back to bed. I did not call you." Samuel was a little confused. He knew he was hearing his name called and if it wasn't Eli calling him, then who was it?

Samuel climbed back into his bed and pulled his blanket up. It took a while for him to fall asleep, because he kept wondering who was calling his name. Just as he was dozing off Samuel heard the voice again, "Samuel! Samuel!" So for the third time Samuel leaped out of bed and ran to Eli.

"What do you need, Sir?" he asked.

At last Eli knew what was going on. **"SAMUEL, IT IS GOD CALLING YOU,"** he told Samuel. "Here's what you do. Go back to bed and when God calls again, say this, 'Here I am.'" Samuel did just what Eli said and God told him amazing things!

SUPER HERO CHARACTERISTIC

Samuel had super-good hearing.
He heard God calling him and
listened to what He said.
A super hero listens carefully
and then acts.

SUPER HERO TIP

It is important to make time to be quiet so you can listen. It's hard to hear God's voice speaking if you don't get quiet first. When you pray, ask God to help you to listen to what He wants to tell you.

"Be still, and know that I am God!"

Psalm 46:10

SUPER HERO DAVID

THE GIANT SLAYER

Based on 1 Samuel 17:19-50

Can a young boy be a super hero? David was! He showed super hero bravery. David's older brothers were soldiers in King Saul's army and David went to visit them. They were camped on a hill across from the Philistine army. One of the Philistine soldiers, a nine-foot tall giant named Goliath, kept shouting at King Saul's army. He shouted bad things about God. He challenged them to send someone out to fight him. But, King Saul's soldiers were all afraid to fight the giant.

David went to King Saul and announced, "I'll fight Goliath." King Saul said, "You're too little. You can't fight him." **BUT DAVID KNEW THAT HE HAD GOD ON HIS SIDE. HE WASN'T SCARED AT ALL.** King Saul gave David his own armor to wear so he would be safer. But it was so big on David that he couldn't even walk.

David took the armor off and grabbed his slingshot and five smooth stones before he headed down the hill to meet the giant. It made Goliath angry to see that a boy was coming to fight him. "Come on," Goliath yelled, "I'll feed you to the birds!"

But David still wasn't scared. He said, "You may have a shield and spear, but I have God on my side. He will help me win!"

David put a stone in his slingshot and swung it around. When he let it go, the stone flew through the air and hit Goliath right in the head. The giant soldier fell to the ground! David had won!

SUPER HERO CHARACTERISTIC

David was brave and fearless. He wasn't afraid of a big and scary giant! He had God on his side.

SUPER HERO TIP

David was not foolish to be so brave. He was brave because he knew that God would help him win the battle. God will help you too. All you have to do is trust Him.

"Don't be afraid, for I am with you. Don't be discouraged, for I am your God. I will strengthen you and help you. I will hold you up with My victorious right hand."

Isaiah 41:10

11

SUPER HERO SOLOMON

A GREAT AND WISE KING

Based on 1 Kings 3

Solomon became king of Israel after his father, David, died. Solomon tried very hard to obey God and live for him. God saw that King Solomon was serious about obeying Him, so He came to Solomon and said, "Ask Me for anything you want and I will give it to you."

Solomon answered, "O God, You have blessed me by making me king of Israel. It is a great responsibility to lead Your people and make good choices for them. So, I ask You to give me wisdom and a heart to understand the people so that I may do a good job leading them. I know that I cannot lead them by myself. I need You to guide me."

God was very pleased that Solomon asked for wisdom and understanding instead of asking for money or to become famous. God answered Solomon's prayer and made him very wise. He also blessed him with lots of money and made him famous.

It wasn't long before Solomon needed the wisdom of God. Two women came to him with a problem. Each of them claimed to be the true mother of a baby boy. "I'm this baby's real mother," one woman said. "She stole him from me during the night."

"She's lying. He's mine!" the other woman cried.

How would the king know which woman was telling the truth? **SOLOMON USED THE WISDOM GOD GAVE HIM.** "Cut the baby in half. Give half to each woman," he ordered. Solomon knew that the real mother would say, "No! Don't hurt him! Let the baby live. She can have him." That's exactly what happened. Now Solomon knew which woman was really the baby's mother.

SUPER HERO CHARACTERISTIC

Solomon was very wise. God gave him the ability to know right from wrong. Solomon used his wisdom to glorify God.

SUPER HERO TIP

When you need wisdom to know right from wrong or to make a good decision, ask God to give you His wisdom. The Bible says that if we ask God for wisdom, He will give it to us.

If you need wisdom, ask our generous God, and He will give it to you.

James 1:5

FIRE FROM HEAVEN

Based on 1 Kings 18:19-40

ELIJAH OBEYED AND SERVED GOD AT A TIME WHEN NOT MANY OTHER PEOPLE DID. In fact, King Ahab and lots of other people served fake gods, like Baal. Things weren't going so well in Israel and King Ahab accused Elijah of causing trouble for everyone who didn't follow God. So Elijah decided it was time to take a stand and make people decide if the fake gods were real or if God was real.

This is how he did it ... he challenged all the priests who followed the fake god Baal to a contest. "Meet me on Mount Carmel. You build an altar and dig a trench around it. Then cut up a bull and put it on the altar, but do not set fire to it. Call for your god, Baal, to send down fire and burn up the offering. Then I will do the same and call on God to burn up the offering."

Baal's priests did what Elijah said. They shouted and called and begged for Baal to send fire. But no fire came. They shouted some more. Elijah watched them. He said, "Maybe Baal is in the bathroom! Shout louder!" They did ... but no fire came.

Finally, Elijah said, "OK, it's my turn." He built an altar and put the bull on it. But he wasn't finished. He wanted to show how very powerful God is. So, he poured lots and lots of water over the altar. Then he called on God to send fire and burn up the offering. God sent fire immediately. He sent such a powerful fire that it burned up the offering and all the water around it. It burned everything!

The prophets of Baal saw the power of the one true God!

SUPER HERO CHARACTERISTIC

Elijah challenged the priests to a contest to see how great their gods were. Elijah won the contest hands down because of course only he served the true and living God who could send down fire from heaven. He wasn't scared of losing against their false gods.

SUPER HERO TIP

Taking a stand for God gives others a chance to see His awesome power! When you serve the one true God you don't have to be afraid of anyone else.

Stand your ground, putting on the belt of truth and the body armor of God's righteousness.

Ephesians 6:14

SUPER HERO DANIEL

13

IN A DEN OF HUNGRY LIONS

Based on Daniel 6

Daniel was just a boy when he became a slave in Babylon. He served God even though he was a slave. God blessed Daniel so that the king noticed him and gave him many gifts. Daniel also became a ruler with two other leaders. The other two didn't think it was right that Daniel was as important as they were. They wanted to get Daniel in trouble with the king. So they looked for things he did wrong that they could complain about. But they couldn't find anything! **DANIEL WAS HONEST AND FAIR AND A HARD WORKER.**

Everyone knew that Daniel's faith in God was very important to him. Daniel's two enemies decided to use that to get him into trouble. They tricked the king into signing a law that said people in the kingdom could not pray to anyone but him. They were sure that Daniel would ignore the law and pray to God as he always did. They were right. Three times a day he knelt in front of an open window and prayed to God!

The two men ran to tell the king that Daniel broke the law. "You have to put him into the lions' den. That's the punishment for breaking the law," they said. The king didn't want to do it. He knew he had been tricked. But he had to obey the law so Daniel was put into the lions' den.

The king stayed awake all night worrying about Daniel. Early the next morning he raced to the lions' den. He was happy to see that God had kept Daniel safe from the lions! Daniel was saved because he did not back down from his faith in God.

SUPER HERO CHARACTERISTIC

Daniel obeyed God with his whole heart and wasn't scared who knew it and what they would do about it. His faith in God was stronger than his fear of what people would do to him.

14

SUPER HERO JONAH

THREE DAYS IN THE BELLY OF A BIG FISH

Based on Jonah 1-4

GOD HAD A SPECIAL JOB FOR JONAH TO DO. He told Jonah to go to Nineveh and tell the people to stop doing bad things and start obeying God. Jonah didn't want to go. He didn't want God to help the people of Nineveh.

Jonah made a bad decision and decided to run away from God! He got on a boat that was going in the opposite direction of Nineveh. Jonah thought he was safe. He even went to sleep.

But Jonah didn't fool God. Before long, God sent a big storm. The little ship was bouncing around in the waves. The sailors were scared that their boat was going to sink. The wind blew harder and harder. Finally they woke up Jonah and asked him if he had any ideas how they could be saved.

Jonah told them that the storm was his fault. He was running from God and God was getting his attention. He told the sailors to toss him overboard and that would make the storm stop. The sailors didn't want to do that, but Jonah told them they had to do it. They picked Jonah up and threw him into the stormy water. Right away God sent a big fish to swallow Jonah right up. God left him inside that fish for three days. Jonah had three days to think about how he had disobeyed God. Finally, he asked God for another chance to obey Him. God made the fish spit Jonah out. Jonah got up and went right to Nineveh to preach about God!

SUPER HERO CHARACTERISTIC

Jonah disobeyed God (not a super hero thing to do), but when God gave him a second chance, he obeyed straight away (a very good super hero thing to do).

SUPER HERO TIP

When you disobey God, tell Him you're sorry and ask for another chance ... then do what He tells you to do!

I will keep on obeying Your instructions forever and ever.

Psalm 119:44

AN APPETITE FOR LOCUSTS AND WILD HONEY

Based on Matthew 3:1-12; Luke 1:5-20

John the Baptist had a very important job. His work was to tell people that Someone more important than him was coming ... Jesus. He didn't go into the cities to tell people this. He stayed out in the wilderness and people came to hear what he was preaching.

The people couldn't miss John! He wore clothes made from camel hair and he ate locusts and wild honey! But they came from all over to hear him say, "Change the way you are living. Pay attention to God."

Many people listened to John's message and decided to change the way they had been living. They decided to stop sinning and to obey God. When they made that decision, John baptized them in the Jordan River.

But John didn't make himself the star of his message. John told people that there was another Man coming whose message was even more important than his. John said, "I am baptizing you with water to show that you have decided to live for God. But the Man coming after me will baptize you with the Holy Spirit! The Spirit will live in your heart and help you live for God!" He was talking about Jesus!

John knew that his work was to help the people get ready to hear all that Jesus would teach them. ***JOHN WAS HAPPY TO DO GOD'S WORK.***

SUPER HERO CHARACTERISTIC

John the Baptist didn't like the limelight and he didn't want to be a superstar. The greatest super heroes are the most humble ones. He knew that Jesus was greater than him and all he wanted to do was prepare the way for the greatest Super Hero of all.

SUPER HERO TIP

God has work for everyone to do.
It's most important to do whatever God
asks you to do – even if you aren't the
"star". You will always be God's star!

God opposes the proud but gives grace to the humble. So humble yourselves under the mighty power of God, and at the right time He will lift you up in honor.

1 Peter 5:5-6

SUPER HERO JESUS

16

AN AWESOME SUPER HERO

Based on Mark 10:13-16

Jesus was becoming more and more famous. Some people followed Him because of the amazing miracles He did – **HEALING SICK PEOPLE, HELPING BLIND PEOPLE SEE AGAIN AND EVEN BRINGING DEAD PEOPLE BACK TO LIFE.** Some people followed Him because they wanted to hear what He taught about loving and obeying God. Big crowds of people followed Jesus everywhere He went.

One thing about Jesus that was different from the religious leaders was that He spent time with people who had diseases that He might catch. Most people didn't do that. He spent time with people who didn't obey God or even care about God. He spent time with the kinds of people that most others did not consider important. Sometimes the religious leaders made fun of Jesus for that. But, He didn't care.

Jesus' own disciples didn't really understand how important every single person was to Him. They just knew that He hardly ever had time to rest. One day some people came to Jesus and brought their young children along. All they wanted was for Jesus to bless their children. But, Jesus' helpers thought that children weren't important enough to take up Jesus' time. They tried to send the children away. They even told the parents that they shouldn't be bothering Jesus with children.

Jesus heard what His followers told the parents and He said, "Stop. Don't send the children away. Let them come to Me. God's kingdom belongs to anyone who has a simple, trusting faith like these children." Jesus took time to bless each of the children who had come!

SUPER HERO CHARACTERISTIC

Jesus is the most awesome Super Hero ever. He did miracles, making blind people see, lame people walk and deaf people hear. He loved everyone and always had time for children.

SUPER HERO TIP

Everyone is important to Jesus. It doesn't matter if they are rich or poor, sick or well. Everyone should be important to you, too! Don't think yourself better than others. Treat others like you would like to be treated.

"Love your neighbor as yourself."
Matthew 22:39

SUPER HERO BOY

17

A SMALL BOY
WITH A SUPER-SIZED LUNCH

Based on John 6:1-14

Thousands of people were near the Sea of Galilee listening to Jesus teaching about living for God. He taught for hours and it was getting late. Finally one of the disciples came to Jesus and said, "Master, You should send these people home to get dinner. It's getting very late and we are far from a town."

"No, I'm not going to send them away," Jesus said, "You give them food." The disciples were surprised that He would say that. He knew that they didn't have any food or any money. Even if they did, there was no place to buy food. So where would they get enough food to feed thousands of people?

The disciples found a young boy who had brought a sack lunch. He had five small loaves of bread and two fish. He generously offered to share his lunch with Jesus. The disciples told Jesus about the boy's offer. But they didn't see what good five loaves of bread and two fish would do when there were more than 5,000 people to feed.

Jesus gladly took the boy's lunch and He thanked God for it. Then He began breaking the loaves of bread into pieces and handing it to His disciples. He did the same with the fish. The disciples were amazed that as He broke the bread and fish there was still more in His hands. Jesus kept handing food to His disciples to pass out to the crowd. More than 5,000 people had all the food they needed that day. **IT ALL STARTED WITH A YOUNG BOY SHARING WHAT HE HAD.**

SUPER HERO CHARACTERISTIC

Wow, imagine your lunch for one turning into a super-duper-sized lunch for 5,000 people! All this happened because a little boy with a little lunch had a big heart for Jesus and for sharing with others.

SUPER HERO TIP

A good way to help others and show your love for God is by sharing what you have with others. He can use your gift, no matter how small you think it is.

Do not forget to do good and to share with others, for with such sacrifices God is pleased.

Hebrews 13:16

MIRACULOUSLY HEALED
AND INCREDIBLY THANKFUL

Based on Luke 17:11-19

Jesus became famous as someone who could heal diseases. More and more people knew about Him. One day, Jesus was traveling to Jerusalem and was about to pass through a small village when He heard someone calling to Him. He looked around and saw ten men standing nearby. They were crying out, "Jesus, please have mercy on us!" All ten of the men had a terrible disease that destroyed their skin. People who had this disease, which was called leprosy, were forced to leave their homes and their families and live in a special camp that was away from other people. This was so that no one else would catch the terrible disease. "Please heal us," the men begged. They wanted to be well again. They wanted to go back to their families.

Jesus just looked at them and said, "Go show yourselves to the priests." That's all He said. That's all He did. As the ten men took off running to see the priests something amazing happened. Miracle of miracles — as they ran, their skin disease began to disappear. They were well! Jesus healed all ten of the men!

Nine men kept right on running to show the priests what had happened to them. But, one man stopped. He turned around and came back to Jesus. **"THANK YOU FOR HEALING ME," SAID THE MAN.**

Jesus said, "I healed ten men. But only one man came to thank Me? What happened to the other nine?" They didn't bother to thank Jesus.

SUPER HERO CHARACTERISTIC

Real super heroes are not afraid to say thank you. The healed leper was a hero because he went back to thank Jesus for his miraculous healing.

SUPER HERO TIP

It is important to thank God for answers to your prayers and for all the wonderful things He does for you – small things and big things!

Give thanks for everything to God the Father in the name of our Lord Jesus Christ.

Ephesians 5:20

SUPER HERO GOOD SAMARITAN

19

ACTION MAN!

Based on Luke 10:25-37

One day a man asked Jesus what he would have to do to know that he would be in heaven someday. Jesus reminded him of the teaching, "Love the Lord your God with all your heart, all your soul, all your strength and all your mind. And, love your neighbor as you love yourself." The man wanted to make his own actions look good so he asked Jesus who he should consider to be his neighbor. Jesus told this story to help the man understand:

"A Jewish man was on his way to Jericho when robbers attacked him and beat him up. They robbed him and even took his clothes, and left him lying on the road to die. Pretty soon a priest came down the road. 'Oh good,' the man thought, 'surely a priest will stop and help me.' But the priest saw the man and crossed the road to get away from him. Later a church worker came down the road, but he stepped over the man and kept on going too. Finally, a man from Samaria came by. Now, everyone knows that Samaritans and Jews didn't like each other. **BUT THIS GOOD SAMARITAN STOPPED AND HELPED THE MAN.** He even took him to an inn and paid the innkeeper to take care of the hurt man until he was well."

Then Jesus turned to the man who had asked the question, "Which man was the real neighbor to the hurt man?"

"The one who helped him," the man answered.

"Yes, so go and live your life in that way," Jesus said.

SUPER HERO CHARACTERISTIC

The Good Samaritan was a man of action. When he saw someone in need, he did something about it. He was helpful and kind.

SUPER HERO TIP

Helping all who need help,
not just your friends,
is an awesome way to show
God's love to others.

Dear children, let's not
merely say that we love each
other; let us show the truth
by our actions.

1 John 3:18

83

20

SUPER HERO FOUR FRIENDS

THE AWESOME FOURSOME

Based on Mark 2:1-12

Jesus was a guest in a house in a small town. News spread quickly that He was there and soon the house was full of people who wanted to hear Him teach. There were four men who heard that Jesus was in town. They had a good friend who was crippled. He couldn't walk. The four friends wanted very much to help their friend. They had heard the stories of when Jesus healed sick people. They believed that if they could get their friend to Jesus, He would heal him too!

The four friends put their crippled friend on a mat and quickly carried him to the house where Jesus was teaching. But it was so crowded that they couldn't even get in the door. The determined friends didn't give up. They believed Jesus could heal their friend if they could just get him inside. They came up with an amazing plan. They carried their friend up to the roof of the house. Then they dug a hole through the roof and lowered their friend on his mat down into the room right in front of Jesus!

JESUS LOOKED UP AT THE FACES OF THE FOUR FRIENDS. HE SAW THE AMAZING FAITH THAT THEY HAD. They truly believed that He could heal their friend. So, Jesus turned to the crippled man and said, "Your sins are forgiven. Get up and walk." Immediately the man got up and walked!

SUPER HERO CHARACTERISTIC

These four friends were an amazing team who had super faith in Jesus. They never gave up until they reached Jesus. They knew He could heal their friend and He did!

SUPER HERO TIP

The four friends had no doubt that Jesus could help their sick friend. Their faith was so strong that they wouldn't give up. They did whatever they had to do to get to Jesus. Have faith, God is always bigger than any problem you face.

Faith is the confidence that what we hope for will actually happen; it gives us assurance about things we cannot see.

Hebrews 11:1

SUPER HERO ZACCHAEUS

21

A LITTLE MAN WITH A BIG HEART

Based on Luke 19:1-10

Zacchaeus was a rich tax collector. No one liked tax collectors because they cheated the people out of their money and kept it for themselves. That's how they got rich. One day Zacchaeus heard that Jesus was coming to his town. He had heard about Jesus and he really wanted to see Him. Zacchaeus went to the street where Jesus was going to pass by, but it was crowded with people. No one would let the tax collector through to the front of the crowd and he was too short to see over the people. So, Zacchaeus climbed up in a tree that was right beside the street. He would be able to see Jesus from there. When Jesus passed by He looked up at the tax collector and said, "Come down, Zacchaeus. I want to come to your house today." Zacchaeus couldn't believe it! He came right down and went to his house with Jesus.

The people were upset that Jesus would spend time with a cheating tax collector! They didn't know that while Jesus and Zacchaeus talked, the little tax collector said, "I'm so sorry that I have cheated people. I will give half of all my money to the poor. And I promise to pay back four times the amount of money I have stolen from people. I won't cheat anyone ever again."

JESUS WAS HAPPY THAT ZACCHAEUS WAS TURNING AWAY FROM DOING WRONG.

He was happy that the tax collector would live for God now.

SUPER HERO CHARACTERISTIC

Zacchaeus might have been a short, greedy little man, but he had a big change of heart after he met Jesus. He changed from being mean and dishonest to being generous and paying back what he owed everyone. That's a super hero change of heart!

SUPER HERO TIP

When you know Jesus, you will be sorry for the wrong things you do. You will turn away from doing those things and turn to Jesus and what He wants you to do. He will help you to do what is right.

If we confess our sins to Him, He is faithful and just to forgive us our sins and to cleanse us from all wickedness.

1 John 1:9

SUPER HERO
PETER

22

WALKING ON WATER!

Based on Matthew 14:22-33

Jesus had been teaching a crowd of people for a long time. He was tired and wanted some time by Himself to rest and pray. So He told His disciples to get in a boat and cross a big lake. He would join them later on the other side of the lake. The disciples did what Jesus told them to do, but in the middle of the night a big storm came up on the lake. The little boat bounced around on the waves and a strong wind blew lots of water into it. The disciples were afraid. They thought their boat was going to sink.

About that time one of them looked out through the rain and blowing water and saw a figure of a man walking through the storm on TOP of the water. At first they were all scared. They thought it was a ghost! But it wasn't a ghost. It was Jesus! "Don't be afraid," He called out to them. "It's Me!"

Peter shouted, "If it's really You, Jesus, let me walk on the water and come to You." Jesus told him to come and **PETER JUMPED RIGHT OUT OF THE BOAT AND WALKED ON TOP OF THE WATER TO JESUS!** But then Peter took his eyes off of Jesus and looked at the big waves and the strong wind. All of that scared him and he sank down into the water. "Aahh, Jesus save me!" he cried. Right away Jesus grabbed his hand and pulled him up. "Oh Peter," Jesus said, "you need to have more faith."

SUPER HERO CHARACTERISTIC

Peter did something humanly impossible – he walked on water! He could only do that because he had faith in Jesus, he stepped out in faith and kept his eyes on Jesus.

SUPER HERO TIP

You can do amazing, unbelievable things if Jesus wants you to. Just step out in faith and keep your eyes on Jesus. Don't let things scare you. Have faith in Him.

When your faith is tested, your endurance has a chance to grow.

James 1:3

SUPER HERO PHILIP

A MAN ON A MISSION

Based on Acts 8:26-40

Philip was an evangelist. That meant that he traveled around teaching people about Jesus. He loved God very much and tried to always obey Him. One day an angel came to talk to Philip and said, "God has a special job for you to do. He wants you to travel down a certain road." Philip didn't know why he should do that, but he obeyed. It wasn't long before a fancy chariot came along. As it passed him, Philip saw the man riding in it. He knew that the man was an important man in the government.

"Go and walk beside the chariot," God told Philip. That's just what he did and he saw that the man was reading from the book of Isaiah.

"Do you understand what you're reading?" Philip asked.

"No. How can I if no one explains it to me?" the man said. "Do you understand it? Can you explain it?" Philip said that he could! So the man invited Philip to ride along with him in the chariot and teach him about God's Word. Philip gladly told the man about God's wonderful love. The man believed everything Philip told him. When he saw a river near the road he asked Philip to baptize him right then and there. The important government man became a Christian because **PHILIP OBEYED GOD AND TOLD THE MAN ABOUT GOD'S LOVE**.

SUPER HERO CHARACTERISTIC

Philip was a man on a mission. His mission was to spread the good news about Jesus. His special assignment was to explain the Bible to the Ethiopian man, who gave his life to Jesus and was baptized - mission accomplished!

SUPER HERO TIP

If you listen for His direction God will give you chances to tell others about God's wonderful love. Be ready to tell others whenever you can!

Go into all the world and preach the gospel to all creation

Mark 16:15

SUPER HERO PAUL

24

A TRUE TRANSFORMER

Based on Acts 9

Paul did NOT like Christians. He did not believe in Jesus. He thought Christians were wrong about what they believed. He even put people in jail just because they followed Jesus. He put all the Christians in his city in jail. Then he got permission to travel to another city to do the same thing. Paul was on his way to a city called Damascus to put the Christians there in jail too. As he walked down the road all of a sudden a very bright light shined down on him and a voice from the sky said, "Paul, why are you doing these things to Me?" Paul was so surprised that he fell flat on the ground.

"Who is this? Who is speaking?" Paul asked.

"I am Jesus," the voice said. The men who were traveling with Paul heard the voice too. But they didn't know where it was coming from. Jesus told Paul to go on into the city and then He would tell him what to do.

When Paul got up, he was blind and had to be led into the city. God told some of the Christians there to take care of Paul. They were afraid because they knew that he put Christians in jail. But, God told them not to be afraid because Paul had changed. Yes, at that very moment when Jesus spoke to him on the road, Paul believed that Jesus is God's Son. He stopped hurting Christians and began following Jesus. **PAUL'S LIFE COMPLETELY CHANGED. HE SPENT THE REST OF HIS LIFE TEACHING OTHERS ABOUT JESUS AND HOW TO LIVE FOR GOD.**

SUPER HERO CHARACTERISTIC

Talk about transformers! Paul was like a real-life transformer! He went from hating Christians to loving Jesus. From being blind to being able to see. From being an agent of darkness to being a radical light spreader.

SUPER HERO TIP

When you believe the truth about Jesus, your life changes – living for God and telling others about Him becomes the most important thing.

Come close to God, and God will come close to you.

James 4:8

25

SUPER HERO JESUS

THE GREATEST, BEST SUPER HERO EVER!

Based on Luke 22:14-20, 39-71; 23:1-56; 24:1-12; John 3:1-21

Many times, as Jesus was teaching, He said that God had sent Him to do something so extraordinary that it would help the whole world.

One evening, Jesus had a special meal with His disciples. Later that night, Jesus asked some of His disciples to go with Him to a garden where He wanted to pray. While He was praying, some angry men came and took Him away. They took Him to their leaders who put Him on trial. Those leaders accused Jesus of things He did not do. They called Him names, treated Him badly and had Him beaten. But Jesus remained silent.

A while later, on a hill outside of the town, Jesus was put on a cross and died. People from all over came and were sad. Jesus' body was taken from the cross and placed in a tomb, closed up by a large stone with soldiers standing guard. Jesus' friends were heartbroken at what they thought was such a terrible end.

Three days later, something amazing happened. The stone at the tomb was rolled back and an angel appeared to tell Jesus' friends that He was not there. Jesus had risen. Soon after, Jesus showed Himself to His friends. He was alive! Jesus had defeated death and proved that He was sent by God to give eternal life to anyone who follows Him. Jesus had said, "God loved the world so much that He gave His one and only Son, so that whoever believes in Him will not die forever, but will have eternal life." Jesus is the Hero of heroes!

SUPER HERO CHARACTERISTIC

Jesus is the greatest Hero the world will ever see. He died on the cross for our sins and He defeated death when He rose from the dead. What a mighty and awesome God He is!

SUPER HERO TIP

Putting others first requires giving up things we think we deserve. Jesus put others first so much that He gave His life for everyone, so that everyone might have eternal life – living with God forever!

God loved the world so much that He gave His one and only Son, so that everyone who believes in Him will not perish but have eternal life.

John 3:16

YOU ARE SPECIAL TO GOD

Do you have a favorite Bible super hero? What do you like about your super hero's story? Do you wonder if you could be a super hero like David or Joshua? Guess what ... you can!

YOU ARE GOD'S OWN SPECIAL SUPER HERO. God has special work that only YOU can do. He will give you His super power to do that work too. Use the courage and strength He gives you to be brave and strong. Use the kind and caring heart He gives you to show others that you care about them and God does too!

God gave you a super hero guidebook. It is the Bible! Read it. Learn it. Remember that you can also ask God for special help anytime you need it.

Do God's work and be a super hero!

Take courage and be a man.

1 Kings 2:2